1

dabblelab

DRAW MANGA
MYTHICAL CREATURES

MANGA DRAWING
WITH DRAGONS, TROLLS, AND OTHER MYTHICAL MONSTERS

written by Naomi Hughes
illustrated by Ludovic Sallé

CAPSTONE PRESS
a capstone imprint

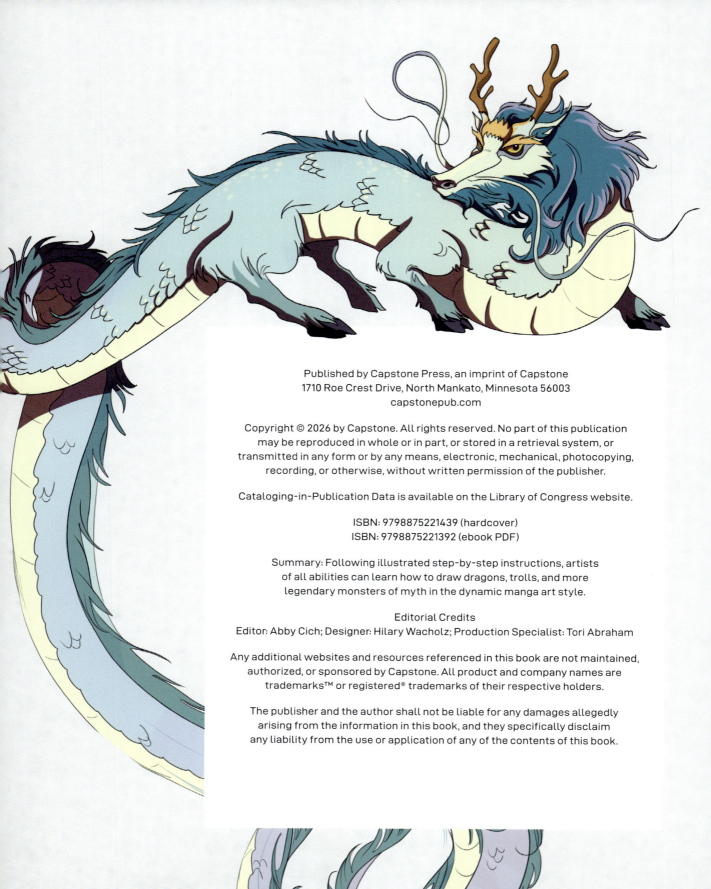

Published by Capstone Press, an imprint of Capstone
1710 Roe Crest Drive, North Mankato, Minnesota 56003
capstonepub.com

Copyright © 2026 by Capstone. All rights reserved. No part of this publication may be reproduced in whole or in part, or stored in a retrieval system, or transmitted in any form or by any means, electronic, mechanical, photocopying, recording, or otherwise, without written permission of the publisher.

Cataloging-in-Publication Data is available on the Library of Congress website.

ISBN: 9798875221439 (hardcover)
ISBN: 9798875221392 (ebook PDF)

Summary: Following illustrated step-by-step instructions, artists of all abilities can learn how to draw dragons, trolls, and more legendary monsters of myth in the dynamic manga art style.

Editorial Credits
Editor: Abby Cich; Designer: Hilary Wacholz; Production Specialist: Tori Abraham

Any additional websites and resources referenced in this book are not maintained, authorized, or sponsored by Capstone. All product and company names are trademarks™ or registered® trademarks of their respective holders.

The publisher and the author shall not be liable for any damages allegedly arising from the information in this book, and they specifically disclaim any liability from the use or application of any of the contents of this book.

Printed and bound in the USA. 006307

TABLE OF CONTENTS

Fierce Legends 4

Supplies 5

Dragon 6

Hydra 8

Troll 10

Manticore 12

Golem 14

Kraken 16

Gorgon 18

Werewolf 20

Yōkai 22

Yeti 24

Vampire 26

A Beastly Battle 28

Draw More Manga Creatures! 32

About the Author 32

About the Illustrator 32

FIERCE LEGENDS

Myths are full of monsters: dragons, yetis, vampires, and more.

Have you ever wanted to draw these creepy critters? Now you can! Even better, you can do it using one of the coolest art forms ever—manga.

Manga is a lot like comics. It tells a story using art. Manga got its start in Japan. But today, it's popular all over the world. From epic adventures to chill slice-of-life stories, manga's got tales for everyone.

Manga art has its own style. Artists draw characters in poses full of action and emotion. They also use special symbols to show mood. Human characters often have large, shiny eyes and small mouths. Don't forget neat hairstyles! Giant hair spikes, bright colors, and more show off spunky personalities. Manga creatures show off, too, with over-the-top features. For cute critters, this can mean big, round faces and sparkly eyes. Monsters are often drawn with lots of angles, like pointy chins and sharp teeth.

Manga is fun and dramatic.
It's perfect for drawing spooky beasts!
And it's time to try it for yourself.

Get ready to draw dragons, trolls, and other mythical monsters . . . MANGA STYLE!

SUPPLIES

Paper. Plain copy paper works well, but many artists use sketch paper.

Pencil. Keep the point sharp (or use a mechanical pencil) and draw lightly. That way, you can easily erase when you need.

Eraser. Because no one draws perfectly all of the time! Plus, manga drawings may take extra practice. Test your eraser first to make sure it doesn't smudge or tear the paper.

Pen. Use a black marker pen with a fine tip or a regular pen. Once you're done with your pencil sketch, trace over it with pen. This will make the lines in your art dark and bold.

Colored markers, colored pencils, or crayons. If you'd like, add color to your art after you've outlined it in pen. Check the ink is dry first so your lines stay crisp.

DID YOU KNOW?
Pro manga artists have special dip pens and ink pots. They use these tools to draw the lines in their final art.

DRAGON

Dragons have been spotted all over the world. In England, they're evil monsters that breathe fire. In China, they're wise guardians. You can find dragons just about anywhere you look. But be careful if you go searching for one! With their powerful bodies and sharp teeth, they're among the most fearsome of monsters.

1

TIP
Dragons come in many colors! Try bright blue, pink and gold, or midnight black. See what you like best.

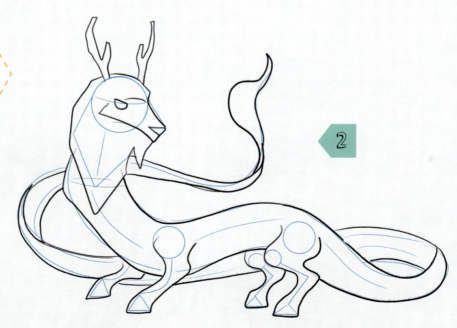

2

6

HYDRA

Even the mighty hero Hercules had trouble slaying one of these monsters. It's easy to see why! Every time a hydra's head is cut off, two more grow back. Not only that, but these creatures have toxic breath and sharp fangs. So, each head is doubly dangerous.

1

FACT
The hydra's middle head is its weak point. If that head is cut off, the hydra will die.

2

TROLL

Trolls are found in dark forests and caves, mainly in Norway. Some are small enough to live under a bridge. Others are as big as mountains. They come in many sizes. But these sturdy creatures all share the same weakness: daylight. A single sunray can turn them to stone.

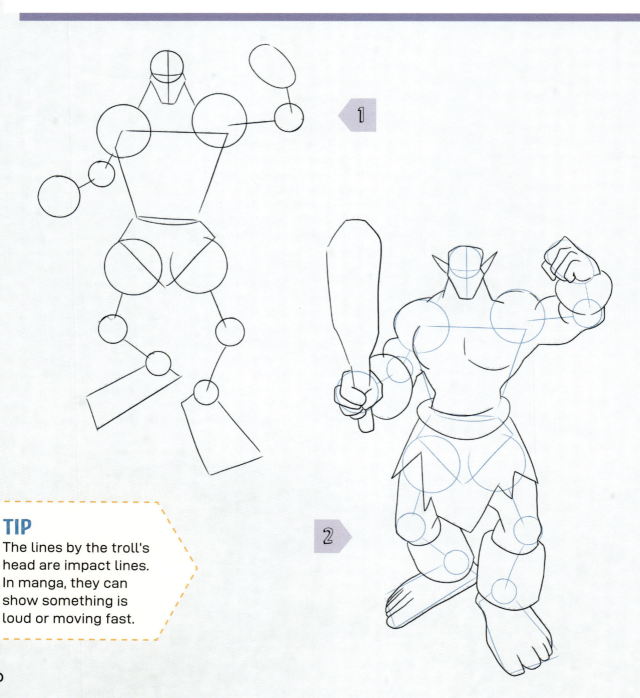

TIP
The lines by the troll's head are impact lines. In manga, they can show something is loud or moving fast.

10

MANTICORE

This beast's name means "man eater." It moves with the strong body of a lion. It strikes with the stinging tail of a scorpion. Even creepier, it has the head (and clever mind) of a human. Few can hope to escape a manticore when it's on the prowl.

FACT
This monster can shoot darts from its tail.

GOLEM

Want to make a golem? All you need to do is shape some clay. Then, add special words to bring it to life. Keep a close eye on your creation, though. Most golems are made to be helpers. But if they stop listening to their creator, their incredible strength can cause giant problems.

TIP
Hands can be tricky to draw! Try looking at your own hand for reference.

Kraken

Sailors beware! The kraken is the king of all sea monsters. This big beast lurks deep under the ocean waves, searching for ships. When the kraken sees one, it surges up to the surface. It easily tears the vessel apart with its strong tentacles.

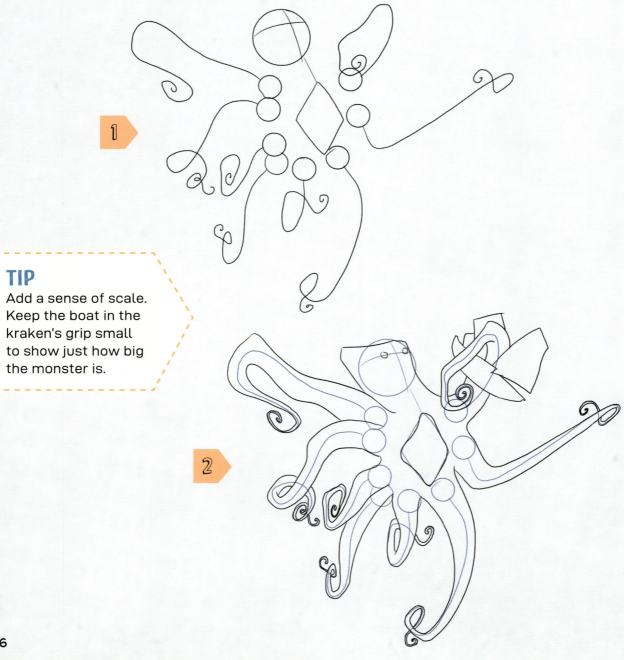

TIP
Add a sense of scale. Keep the boat in the kraken's grip small to show just how big the monster is.

GORGON

Long ago in Greece, three special sisters were born. They are the gorgons. Their hair wriggles with snakes. One look at them can turn a person into stone. Because of these scary traits, many stories say the gorgons are evil. But are they really? Ask one yourself . . . just make sure to wear a blindfold!

TIP
Poses help show attitude. This action pose makes the gorgon look fierce!

18

WEREWOLF

Most of the time, werewolves seem like normal people. But on the night of the full moon, be on guard. That's when they change into their wolf forms. Some werewolves can still think clearly while they're shifted. Others are not so lucky. They become monsters in both body and mind.

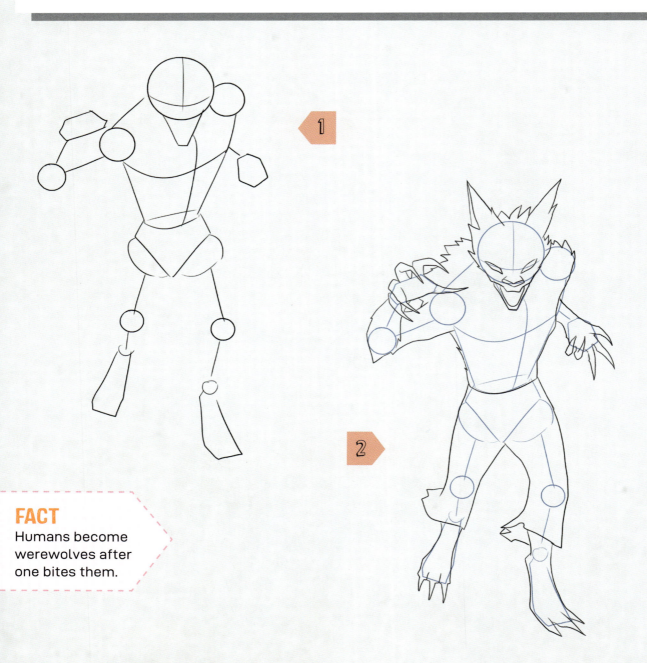

FACT
Humans become werewolves after one bites them.

20

YŌKAI

There's nothing nicer than a stroll on the beach . . . unless this creepy-crawly is waiting beneath the waves. This ox-spider mash-up is a type of yōkai, or Japanese demon. Some yōkai are friendly to humans. This one likes to eat them. It hunts near the water. So be careful the next time you go swimming!

FACT
There are lots of different yōkai. This one is called Ushi-oni.

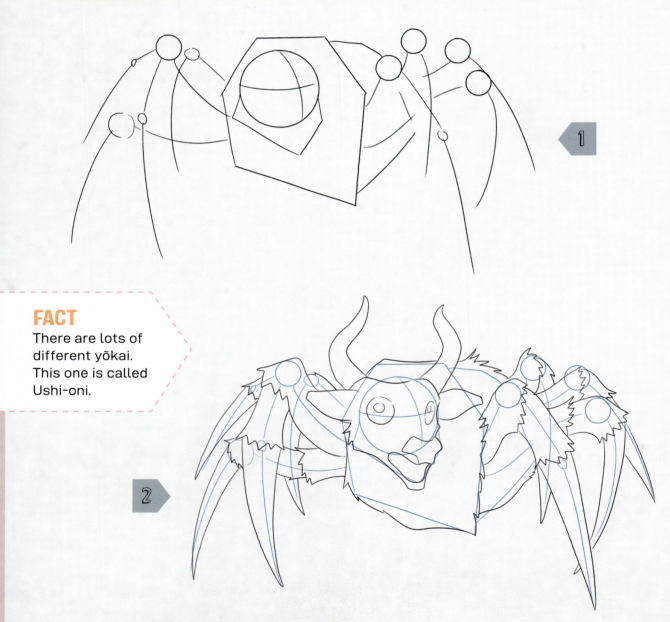

22

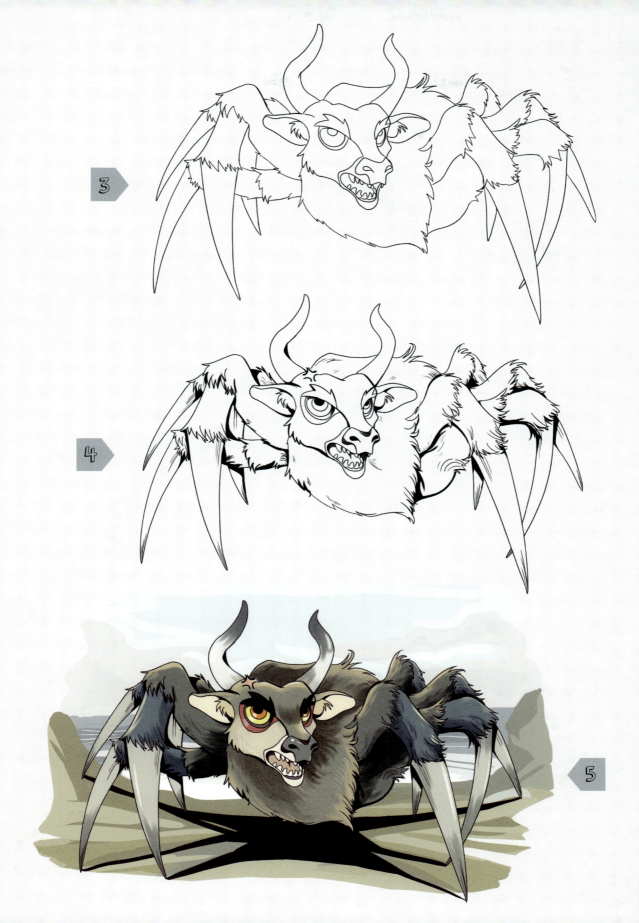

YETI

Many brave explorers have searched for yetis in the snowy mountains of Tibet. Some people return telling tales of an ape-like creature on the slopes. Others come back with photos of footprints. And a few never return at all. Did they fall victim to the yeti? We may never know.

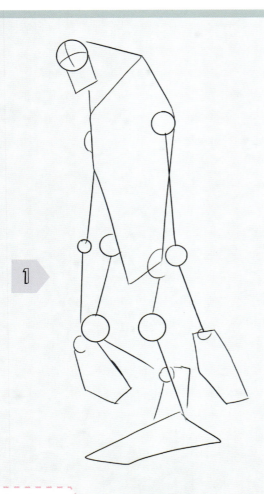

1

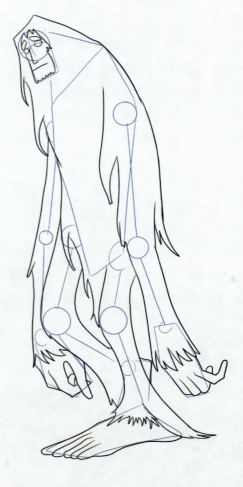

2

FACT
Yetis can have white fur. This makes them hard to see in the snow.

24

VAMPIRE

Vampires might be the most legendary monsters. These creatures of the night are found in shadows worldwide. They stalk the darkness with their fangs bared as they hunt for their next victim. Some can turn into bats. Others have super strength. One thing they all have in common? Human blood is their favorite meal.

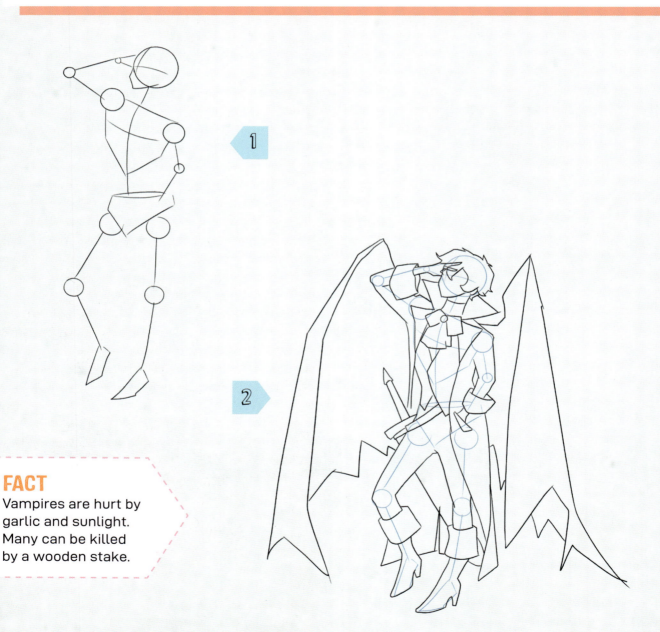

FACT
Vampires are hurt by garlic and sunlight. Many can be killed by a wooden stake.

A Beastly Battle

Watch out! Both a dragon and a troll want to make their home in the same rocky terrain. There's only room for one big brute, though. Will the master of the air come out on top? Or will it be the terror of the earth? Whoever wins, this mythical battle will be a scene to remember!

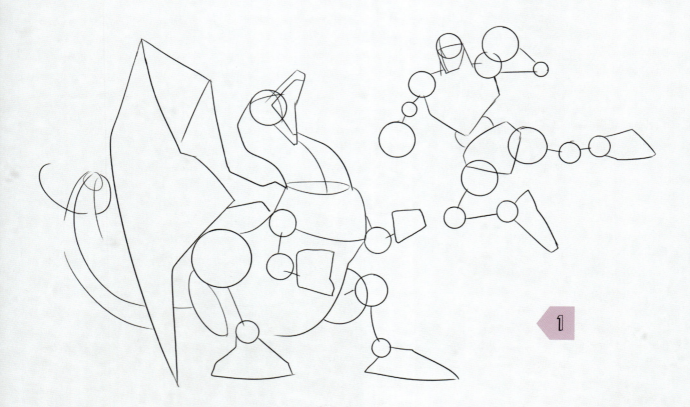

TIP

See the yellow mark by the troll's head? That is a kind of manpu. In manga, these special symbols help show a character's feelings. This one shows anger.

DRAW MORE MANGA CREATURES!

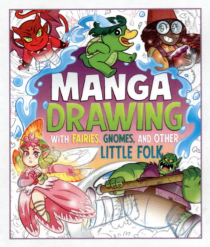
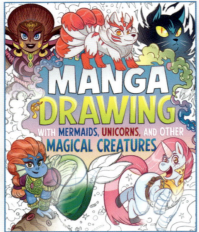
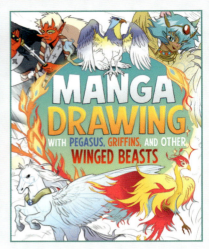

ABOUT THE AUTHOR

Naomi Hughes is an author and school librarian in Minnesota, where she lives with her family and a house full of pets. She writes all sorts of books for kids, from nonfiction picture books to science fiction and fantasy for teens. She loves all things manga and anime and also enjoys traveling, reading, escape games, and going on adventures.

ABOUT THE ILLUSTRATOR

Ludovic Sallé is a French artist who enjoys working both traditionally with watercolor and acrylic, as well as digitally. His manga-inspired style allows him to explore a dynamic, colorful graphic universe and to create cute characters.